JAMES ALLEN: A PROPHET OF MEDITATION

Although the late James Allen, of Ilfracombe, is comparatively unknown, yet to thousands of seekers after truth, he has proved a guide, philosopher, and friend. One of his works, "As a Man Thinketh", has gone into no less than eleven editions; surely proof that he has a considerable vogue. The most casual reader of any of his works cannot fail to be impressed by the simplicity, cheerfulness, and benevolence which seem to radiate from the soul of the writer. We cannot place James Allen in any exclusive category, as he teaches so much that harmonizes with all the best thought of our age. Liberal Christians, Theosophists, and many other enlightened bodies of truth-seekers may claim him as an exponent of at least several of their distinctive views; be he was simply a strong, true, individual man who wrote and spoke out of the depth of his own convictions, and never held himself bound to voice the peculiar tenets of any cult. Wide knowledge of the Scriptures of the world, professedly sacred and other, coupled with intense sympathy with all human causes have rendered his works a delight to the scholar, as well as an inspiration to the less cultured aspirant for instruction in that path of wisdom which inevitably leads to power and peace. His literary style is clear and simple, and in dealing with subjects that are often vague and illusory, he used language that made his meaning easily understood. James Allen disliked publicity, and, perhaps, it is because of his disregard of the uses of advertisement that he is not so well known as he might otherwise have been. After all, however, it is the man's message that matters, and he who runs may read in the James Allen Library the story of the spiritual life of the writer. The worship of the personality was a thing that he always guarded against, and for that reason his body was cremated and his ashes scattered to the four winds of Heaven, so that no man or woman in the future could make a place of pilgrimage of his grave, or say "the dust of James Allen lies here.: His books alone are monuments to his memory, and they are being sent with the utmost speed to all the corners of the earth, and are being translated into various languages. "The Eight Pillars of Prosperity" has just been published in the Spanish tongue.

James Allen was born in Leicester on November 28th, 1864. His father was at one time a very prosperous manufacturer, but evil days overtook him when James was about fifteen years of age. Nearly everything was lost, and Allen, senior, taking what money was left, went to America to make a new home for his wife and family, but within two days of his arrival in that country he met with an accident and died in a New York hospital. His empty pocket-book and an old silver watch were returned to the family as the only things found upon him. James now found himself in his native town of Leicester, at the age of fifteen, with a mother and two younger brothers to support. He

1

worked as many as fifteen hours a day in a factory, but never gave up his beloved books.

Mr. Allen states that at the age of seventeen, he found his father's Shakespeare, of which he became an ardent reader. "I read Shakespeare," he himself has said, "in the early morning, at breakfast time, in the dinner hour, and in the evening." He knew the whole of the plays by heart ultimately, and could lose himself in them when surrounded by hundreds of workmen and by the whir and thud of machinery.

Then came Emerson's Essays, calm and radiant, revealing to him a higher realm than that of the passions with their fleeting pleasures and certain pains. "Circles," "Compensation," "The Over-Soul," and "Self Reliance" were the essays which impressed him most, particularly "Self Reliance," which showed him the importance of conduct and the worth and dignity of character. It helped him to battle successfully with natural timidity, which put a check on initiative and originality.

Then, at age 23, he came across Sir Edwin Arnold's "The Light of Asia." Describing his sensations after reading it, he has said, "I could not stir from my seat till I read every word. When I did rise from the reading of this book, it was as though I had become a different man. A curtain seemed to have rolled back from the face of the Universe, and I saw the causes and meaning of things which had hitherto been dark mysteries. There was a revelation which was almost blending in its brilliance and suddenness, an exaltation which alarmed me while it transported me into a felicitous insight. The vision quickly faded, but its influence remained, the memory of it saving me in many an hour of darkness and temptation, until that calmer time of meditation and knowledge, ten years later, when it returned never again to fade from the mind." In "The Light of Asia," Sir Edwin Arnold sought, by the medium of an imaginary Buddhist votary, to depict the life and character and indicate the philosophy of that noble hero and reformer, Prince Gautama of India, the founder of Buddhism. "More than a third of mankind owe their moral and religious ideas to this illustrious prince, whose personality, though imperfectly revealed in the existing sources of information, cannot but appear the highest, gentlest, holiest, and most beneficent, which one exception, in the history of Thought."

> If ye lay bound upon the wheel of change,
> And no way were of breaking from the chain,
> The Heart of boundless Being is a curse,
> The soul of thing fell pain.
> Ye are not bound! The soul of things is sweet,
> The heart of being is celestial rest;
> Stronger than woe is will; that which was good
> Doth pass to better —best.

I, Buddha, who wept with all my brother's tears,
Whose heart was broken by a whole world's woe,
Laugh and am glad, for there is liberty!
Ho! Ye who suffer! Know.
Ye suffer from yourselves. None else compels,
None other holds you that ye live and die,
And whirl upon the wheel, and hug and kiss
It spokes of agony.
Its tire of tears, its nave of nothingness,
Behold, I show you Truth! Lower than hell,
Higher than heaven, outside the utmost stars,
Farther than Brahm doth dwell.
Before beginning, and without an end,
As space eternal and as surety sure,
Is fixed a power divine which moves to good,
Only its laws endure.

From the date of reading "The Light of Asia" began James Allen's great search for truth.

At the age of 26 came "The Bhagavad Gita." There followed the books of the Chinese sages and the Gospel of Buddha by Paul Carus, Dr. Bucke's Cosmic Conservances also had an influence on him, inasmuch as it gave a scientific explanation of what had already been revealed inwardly.

When about the age of 25, James Allen left his native town and went to London, where he was for a time a private secretary, working from 9 to 6 o'clock, and using every moment out of office hours for writing his books. He afterwards founded "The Light of Reason," and gave up his time to the work of editing the magazine, at the same time carrying on a voluminous correspondence with searchers after truth all over the world. He met Mrs. Allen, who was a sister in an East End mission at the time, when he was 29 years of age. She proved a true mate, and now carries on the work which her husband inaugurated. Leaving London, they took up residence in beautiful Ilfracombe, where the remainder of James Allen's life was spent.

His first book was "From Poverty to Power," which is considered to be his best work. It has passed into many editions, and Mrs. Allen states that tens of thousands have been sold all over the world, both authorized and pirated editions. In this book he urges the reader to strive to realize, and merely hold as a theory, the evil is a passing phase, a self-created shadow; that all your pains, sorrows, and misfortunes have come to you by a process of undeviating and absolutely perfect law; have come to you because you deserve and require them, and that by first enduring, and then understanding them, you may be made stronger, wiser, nobler. He says: "When you have fully entered into his realization, you will be in a position to mould your own circumstances, to transmute all evil into good, and to weave, with a master hand, the fabric of your destiny." Soon after the publication of "From Poverty to Power," came "All These Things Added," and then, "As a Man Thinketh." Other books followed such as "Above Life's Turmoil," "The Mastery of Destiny," "Byways of Blessedness," "The Life Triumphant," "Out From the Heart," "Through the Gate of Good," "From Passion to Peace," "Man: King of Mind, Body, and Circumstance," and "The Eight Pillars of Prosperity." James Allen took a keen interest in many scientific subjects, delighting in astronomy, geology, and botany, and might have written on a wide range of subjects had he chosen to do so. He was often asked for articles on many question outside his own particular work, but he refused to comply, concentrating his whole though and effort on preaching the gospel of selflessness. After a short illness, he died on January 24th, 1912, in the forty-eighth year of his age. Six days later his remains were cremated at Leicester, and his ashes were devoutly scattered to the four winds with the following invocation, uttered audibly:

"As these ashes of James Allen are cast to the four winds of heaven, so may the truth he taught permeate to the four corners of the earth, carrying with it joy, peace, and consolation."

Although what James Allen taught may not be new —old truth in a new setting- yet the direct and forceful style in which he expressed his thoughts undoubtedly give him a special niche among ethical writers. His magazine, "The Light of Reason," was founded in 1902. It took hold of a large number of the thinking public at once, and its usefulness was assured. Immediately upon its publication, letters began to pour in from all parts of the kingdom, from all sorts and conditions of men and women asking for advice, for spiritual help and guidance. Later, when the magazine found its way to America, New Zealand, India, and the Far East, the correspondence became so heavy the for hours every day Mr. Allen did nothing but answer letters. In 1905 he established The Brotherhood, or School of Virtue, the central doctrine of which is the renunciation of self for the good of the world, and necessarily its corollary, the practice of divine love towards all creatures and beings. The rules of the Brotherhood are those principles of truth which the seekers after righteousness in all ages have adopted. Religions change from age to age, but the principles of divine virtue are eternally the same, and these principles are embodied in the rules of the Brotherhood. In June, 1910, "The Epoch" was started. With it is incorporated "The Light of Reason." It is edited by Mrs. Allen, and has a large and increasing sale in all parts of the world.

I have called James Allen a prophet of meditation, because meditation was one of the chief things he emphasized in his writings. He always urged that each man must learn the truth for himself. Reading books and accepting what is said as you may accept the food that is before you, is not enough. He points out in his book, "The Mastery of Destiny," that aspiration must be united to concentration, the result being meditation. When a man intensely desires to reach and realize a higher, purer, and more radiant life than the merely worldly and pleasure-loving life, he engages in aspiration, and when he earnestly concentrates his thoughts upon the finding of that life, he practices meditation.

Without intense aspiration, there can be no meditation. The more intense nature of a man, the more readily will he practice it. The meditative life is a child of the East, and though both preached and practiced by the Master, it is made conspicuous to-day by its absence from the habit of the great majority of religious people. The men who have had most influence in the world have been the spiritually developed men, and, therefore, spiritual development ought to be our chief aim. Spiritual development can only be obtained by meditation, which consist in bringing the mind to a focus in its search for the Divine knowledge, the Divine life; the intense dwelling in thought on Truth. The object of mediation is Diving enlightenment, the attainment, of truth, and is, therefore, interwoven with practical purity and righteousness. Thus, while at first the time spent in actual meditation is short –perhaps only half-an-hour in the early morning –the knowledge gained in that half-hour of vivid aspiration and concentration though is embodied in practice during the whole day. In meditation, therefore, the entire life of a man is involved; and as he advances in practice he becomes more and more fitted to perform the duties of life in the circumstances in which he may be placed, for he becomes stronger, holier, calmer, and wiser.

Many people think they are meditating when they are simply indulging in reverie or a brown study. This is fatal error. James Allen points out that reverie is a loose dreaming into which a man falls: meditation is a strong, purposeful thinking into which a man rises. Reverie is easy and pleasurable; meditation is a first difficult and irksome. Reverie thrives in indolence and luxury; meditation arises from strenuousness and discipline. Reverie is first alluring, then sensuous, and then sensual. Meditation is first forbidding, then profitable, and then peaceful. Reverie is dangerous, it undermines self-control. Meditation is protective, it establishes self-control.

Now, James Allen shows that there are certain signs by which one can know whether he is engaging in reverie or meditation, and I think these will prove of interest. The indications of reverie are: A desire to avoid exertion; a desire to experience the pleasure of dreaming; an increasing distaste for one's worldly duties; a desire to shirk one's worldly responsibilities; fear of consequences; a wish to get money with as little effort as possible; lack of self-control. The indications of meditation are: Increase of both physical and mental energy; a strenuous striving after wisdom; a decrease in irksomeness in the performance of duty; a fixed determination to fulfill faithfully all worldly responsibilities; freedom from fear; indifference to riches; possession of self-control.

Of course, meditation is not possible under certain circumstances. The time, places and conditions in which James Allen considered meditation impossible are as follow: At, or immediately after, meals; in paces of pleasure; in crowded places; while walking rapidly; while lying in bed in the morning; while smoking. Here is a list of times, places, and conditions in which meditation is difficult: At night; in a luxuriously furnished room; while sitting on a soft, yielding seat; while wearing gay apparel; when in company; when the body is weary; if the body is given too much food.

The times, places, and conditions in which it is best to meditate are: Very early in the morning; immediately before meals; in solitude, in the open air, or in a plainly furnished room; while sitting on a hard seat; when the body is strong and vigorous; when the body is modestly and plainly clothed. The difficulty, of course, with the beginner is how to set about the practice of meditation. He may get up in the morning to meditate, but presently his mind drifts on to one thing and another. Aspiration can often best be aroused and the mind renewed in meditation by the mental repetition of a lofty precept, a beautiful sentence, or a verse of poetry. Indeed, the mind that is ready for meditation will instinctively adopt this practice.

Murdo S. Carruthers

From Herald of the Star, March 1916.

THE PATH TO PROSPERITY
1. THE LESSON OF EVIL

Unrest and pain and sorrow are the shadows of life. There is no heart in all the world that has not felt the sting of pain, no mind has not been tossed upon the dark waters of trouble, no eye that has not wept the hot blinding tears of unspeakable anguish.

There is no household where the Great Destroyers, disease and death, have not entered, severing heart from heart, and casting over all the dark pall of sorrow. In the strong, and apparently indestructible meshes of evil all are more or less fast caught, and pain, unhappiness, and misfortune wait upon mankind.

With the object of escaping, or in some way mitigating this overshadowing gloom, men and women rush blindly into innumerable devices, pathways by which they fondly hope to enter into a happiness which will not pass away.

Such are the drunkard and the harlot, who revel in sensual excitements; such is the exclusive aesthete, who shuts himself out from the sorrows of the world, and surrounds himself with enervating luxuries; such is he who thirsts for wealth or fame, and subordinates all things to the achievement of that object; and such are they who seek consolation in the performance of religious rites.

And to all the happiness sought seems to come, and the soul, for a time, is lulled into a sweet security, and an intoxicating forgetfulness of the existence of evil; but the day of disease comes at last, or some great sorrow, temptation, or misfortune breaks suddenly in on the unfortified soul, and the fabric of its fancied happiness is torn to shreds.

So over the head of every personal joy hangs the Damocletian sword of pain, ready, at any moment, to fall and crush the soul of him who is unprotected by knowledge.

The child cries to be a man or woman; the man and woman sigh for the lost felicity of childhood. The poor man chafes under the chains of poverty by which he is bound, and the rich man often lives in fear of poverty, or scours the world in search of an elusive shadow he calls happiness.

Sometimes the soul feels that it has found a secure peace and happiness in adopting a certain religion, in embracing an intellectual philosophy, or in building up an intellectual or artistic ideal; but some overpowering temptation proves the religion to be inadequate or insufficient; the theoretical philosophy is found to be a useless prop; or in a moment, the idealistic statue upon which the devotee has for years been laboring, is shattered into fragments at his feet.

Is there, then, no way of escape from pain and sorrow? Are there no means by which bonds of evil may be broken? Is permanent happiness, secure prosperity, and abiding peace a foolish dream?

No, there is a way, and I speak it with gladness, by which evil can be slain for ever; there is a process by which disease, poverty, or any adverse condition or circumstance can be put on one side never to return; there is a method by which a permanent prosperity can be secured, free from all fear of the return of adversity, and there is a practice by which unbroken and unending peace and bliss can be partaken of and realized.

And the beginning of the way which leads to this glorious realization is the acquirement of a right understanding of the nature of evil.

It is not sufficient to deny or ignore evil; it must be understood. It is not enough to pray to God to remove the evil; you must find out why it is there, and what lesson it has for you.

It is of no avail to fret and fume and chafe at the chains which bind you; you must know why and how you are bound. Therefore, reader, you must get outside yourself, and must begin to examine and understand yourself.

You must cease to be a disobedient child in the school of experience and must begin to learn, with humility and patience, the lessons that are set for your edification and ultimate perfection; for evil, when rightly understood, is found to be, not an unlimited power or principle in the universe, but a passing phase of human experience, and it therefore becomes a teacher to those who are willing to learn.

Evil is not an abstract some thing outside yourself; it is an experience in your own heart, and by patiently examining and rectifying your heart you will be gradually led into the discovery of the origin and nature of evil, which will necessarily be followed by its complete eradication.

All evil is corrective and remedial, and is therefore not permanent. It is rooted in ignorance, ignorance of the true nature and relation of things, and so long as we remain in that state of ignorance, we remain subject to evil.

There is no evil in the universe which is not the result of ignorance, and which would not, if we were ready and willing to learn its lesson, lead us to higher wisdom, and then vanish away. But men remain in evil, and it does not pass away because men are not willing or prepared to learn the lesson which it came to teach them.

I knew a child who, every night when its mother took it to bed, cried to be allowed to play with the candle; and one night, when the mother was off guard for a moment, the child took hold of the candle; the inevitable result followed, and the child never wished to play with the candle again.

By its one foolish act it learned, and learned perfectly the lesson of obedience, and entered into the knowledge that fire burns. And, this incident is a complete illustration of the nature, meaning, and ultimate result of all sin and evil.

As the child suffered through its own ignorance of the real nature of fire, so older children suffer through their ignorance of the real nature of the things which they weep for and strive after, and which harm them when they are secured; the only difference being that in the latter case the ignorance and evil are more deeply rooted and obscure.

Evil has always been symbolized by darkness, and Good by light, and hidden within the symbol is contained the perfect interpretation, the reality; for, just as light always floods the universe, and darkness is only a mere speck or shadow cast by a small body intercepting a few rays of the illimitable light, so the Light of the Supreme Good is the positive and life-giving power which floods the universe, and evil the insignificant shadow cast by the self that intercepts and shuts off the illuminating rays which strive for entrance.

When night folds the world in its black impenetrable mantle, no matter how dense the darkness, it covers but the small space of half our little planet, while the whole universe is ablaze with living light, and every soul knows that it will awake in the light in the morning.

Know, then, that when the dark night of sorrow, pain, or misfortune settles down upon your soul, and you stumble along with weary and uncertain steps, that you are merely intercepting your own personal desires between yourself and the boundless light of joy and bliss, and the dark shadow that covers you is cast by none and nothing but yourself.

And just as the darkness without is but a negative shadow, an unreality which comes from nowhere, goes to nowhere, and has no abiding dwelling place, so the darkness within is equally a negative shadow passing over the evolving and Lightborn soul.

"But," I fancy I hear someone say, "why pass through the darkness of evil at all?" Because, by ignorance, you have chosen to do so, and because, by doing so, you may understand both good and evil, and may the more appreciate the light by having passed through the darkness.

As evil is the direct outcome of ignorance, so, when the lessons of evil are fully learned, ignorance passes away, and wisdom takes its place. But as a disobedient child refuses to learn its lessons at school, so it is possible to refuse to learn the lessons of experience, and thus to remain in continual darkness, and to suffer continually recurring punishments in the form of disease, disappointment, and sorrow.

He, therefore, who would shake himself free of the evil which encompasses him, must be willing and ready to learn, and must be prepared to undergo that disciplinary process without which no grain of wisdom or abiding happiness and peace can be secured.

A man may shut himself up in a dark room, and deny that the light exists, but it is everywhere without, and darkness exists only in his own little room.

So you may shut out the light of Truth, or you may begin to pull down the walls of prejudice, self-seeking and error which you have built around yourself, and so let in the glorious and omnipresent Light.

By earnest self-examination strive to realize, and not merely hold as a theory, that evil is a passing phase, a self-created shadow; that all your pains, sorrows and misfortunes have come to you by a process of undeviating and absolutely perfect law; have come to you because you deserve and require them, and that by first enduring, and then understanding them, you may be made stronger, wiser, nobler.

When you have fully entered into this realization, you will be in a position to mould your own circumstances, to transmute all evil into good and to weave, with a master hand, the fabric of your destiny.

What of the night, O Watchman! see'st thou yet
The glimmering dawn upon the mountain heights,
The golden Herald of the Light of lights,
Are his fair feet upon the hilltops set?
Cometh he yet to chase away the gloom,
And with it all the demons of the Night?
Strike yet his darting rays upon thy sight?
Hear'st thou his voice, the sound of error's doom?
The Morning cometh, lover of the Light;
Even now He gilds with gold the mountain's brow,
Dimly I see the path whereon even now
His shining feet are set toward the Night.
Darkness shall pass away, and all the things
That love the darkness, and that hate the Light
Shall disappear for ever with the Night:
Rejoice! for thus the speeding Herald sings.

2. THE WORLD A REFLEX OF MENTAL STATES

What you are, so is your world. Everything in the universe is resolved into your own inward experience. It matters little what is without, for it is all a reflection of your own state of consciousness.

It matters everything what you are within, for everything without will be mirrored and colored accordingly.

All that you positively know is contained in your own experience; all that you ever will know must pass through the gateway of experience, and so become part of yourself.

Your own thoughts, desires, and aspirations comprise your world, and, to you, all that there is in the universe of beauty and joy and bliss, or of ugliness and sorrow and pain, is contained within yourself.

By your own thoughts you make or mar your life, your world, your universe, As you build within by the power of thought, so will your outward life and circumstances shape themselves accordingly.

Whatsoever you harbor in the inmost chambers of your heart will, sooner or later by the inevitable law of reaction, shape itself in your outward life.

The soul that is impure, sordid and selfish, is gravitating with unerring precision toward misfortune and catastrophe; the soul that is pure, unselfish, and noble is gravitating with equal precision toward happiness and prosperity.

Every soul attracts its own, and nothing can possibly come to it that does not belong to it. To realize this is to recognize the universality of Divine Law.

The incidents of every human life, which both make and mar, are drawn to it by the quality and power of its own inner thought-life. Every soul is a complex combination of gathered experiences and thoughts, and the body is but an improvised vehicle for its manifestation.

What, therefore, your thoughts are, that is your real self; and the world around, both animate and inanimate, wears the aspect with which your thoughts clothe it.

"All that we are is the result of what we have thought. It is founded on our thoughts; it is made up of our thoughts." Thus said Buddha, and it therefore follows that if a man is happy, it is because he dwells in happy thoughts; if miserable, because he dwells in despondent and debilitating thoughts,

Whether one be fearful or fearless, foolish or wise, troubled or serene, within that soul lies the cause of its own state or states, and never without. And now I seem to hear a chorus of voices exclaim, "But do you really mean to say that outward circumstances do not affect our minds?" I do not say that, but I say this, and know it to be an infallible truth, that circumstances can only affect you in so far as you allow them to do so.

You are swayed by circumstances because you have not a right understanding of the nature, use, and power of thought.

You believe (and upon this little word belief hang all our sorrows and joys) that outward things have the power to make or mar your life; by so doing you submit to those outward things, confess that you are their slave, and they your unconditional master; by so doing, you invest them with a power which they do not, of themselves, possess, and you succumb, in reality, not to the mere circumstances, but to the gloom or gladness, the fear or hope, the strength or weakness, which your thought-sphere has thrown around them.

I knew two men who, at an early age, lost the hard-earned savings of years. One was very deeply troubled, and gave way to chagrin, worry, and despondency.

The other, on reading in his morning paper that the bank in which his money was deposited had hopelessly failed, and that he had lost all, quietly and firmly remarked, "Well, it's gone, and trouble and worry won't bring it back, but hard work will."

He went to work with renewed vigor, and rapidly became prosperous, while the former man, continuing to mourn the loss of his money, and to grumble at his "bad luck," remained the sport and tool of adverse circumstances, in reality of his own weak and slavish thoughts.

The loss of money was a curse to the one because he clothed the event with dark and dreary thoughts; it was a blessing to the other, because he threw around it thoughts of strength, of hope, and renewed endeavor.

If circumstances had the power to bless or harm, they would bless and harm all men alike, but the fact that the same circumstances will be alike good and bad to different souls proves that the good or bad is not in the circumstance, but only in the mind of him that encounters it.

When you begin to realize this you will begin to control your thoughts, to regulate and discipline your mind, and to rebuild the inward temple of your soul, eliminating all useless and superfluous material, and incorporating into your being thoughts alone of joy and serenity, of strength and life, of compassion and love, of beauty and immortality; and as you do this you will become joyful and serene, strong and healthy, compassionate and loving, and beautiful with the beauty of immortality.

And as we clothe events with the drapery of our own thoughts, so likewise do we clothe the objects of the visible world around us, and where one sees harmony and beauty, another sees revolting ugliness.

An enthusiastic naturalist was one day roaming the country lanes in pursuit of his hobby, and during his rambles came upon a pool of brackish water near a farmyard.

As he proceeded to fill a small bottle with the water for the purpose of examination under the microscope, he dilated, with more enthusiasm than discretion, to an uncultivated son of the plough who stood close by, upon the hidden and innumerable wonders contained in the pool, and concluded by saying, "Yes, my friend, within this pool is contained a hundred, nay, a million universes, had we but the sense or the instrument by which we could apprehend them." And the unsophisticated one ponderously remarked, "I know the water be full o' tadpoles, but they be easy to catch."

Where the naturalist, his mind stored with the knowledge of natural facts, saw beauty, harmony, and hidden glory, the mind unenlightened upon those things saw only an offensive mud-puddle.

The wild flower which the casual wayfarer thoughtlessly tramples upon is, to the spiritual eye of the poet, an angelic messenger from the invisible.

To the many, the ocean is but a dreary expanse of water on which ships sail and are sometimes wrecked; to the soul of the musician it is a living thing, and he hears, in all its changing moods, divine harmonies.

Where the ordinary mind sees disaster and confusion, the mind of the philosopher sees the most perfect sequence of cause and effect, and where the materialist sees nothing but endless death, the mystic sees pulsating and eternal life.

And as we clothe both events and objects with our own thoughts, so likewise do we clothe the souls of others in the garments of our thoughts.

The suspicious believe everybody to be suspicious; the Liar feels secure in the thought that he is not so foolish as to believe that there is such a phenomenon as a strictly truthful person; the envious see envy in every soul; the miser thinks everybody is eager to get his money; he who has subordinated conscience in the making of his wealth, sleeps with a revolver under his pillow, wrapped in the delusion that the world is full of conscienceless people who are eager to rob him, and the abandoned sensualist looks upon the saint as a hypocrite.

On the other hand, those who dwell in loving thoughts, see that in all which calls forth their love and sympathy; the trusting and honest are not troubled by suspicions; the good-natured and charitable who rejoice at the good fortune of others, scarcely know what envy means; and he who has realized the Divine within himself recognizes it in all beings, even in the beasts.

And men and women are confirmed in their mental outlook because of the fact that, by the law of cause and effect, they attract to themselves that which they send forth, and so come in contact with people similar to themselves.

The old adage, "Birds of a feather flock together," has a deeper significance than is generally attached to it, for in the thought-world as in the world of matter, each clings to its kind.

Do you wish for kindness? Be kind.
Do you ask for truth? Be true.

What you give of yourself you find;
Your world is a reflex of you.

If you are one of those who are praying for, and looking forward to, a happier world beyond the grave, here is a message of gladness for you, you may enter into and realize that happy world now; it fills the whole universe, and it is within you, waiting for you to find, acknowledge, and possess. Said one who knew the inner laws of Being,"

When men shall say Io here, or Io there, go not after them; the kingdom of God is within you."

What you have to do is to believe this, simply believe it with a mind unshadowed by doubt, and then meditate upon it till you understand it.

You will then begin to purify and to build your inner world, and as you proceed, passing from revelation to revelation, from realization to realization, you will discover the utter powerlessness of outward things beside the magic potency of a self-governed soul.

If thou would'st right the world,
And banish all its evils and its woes,
Make its wild places bloom,
And its drear deserts blossom as the rose,-
Then right thyself.
If thou would'st turn the world
From its long, lone captivity in sin,
Restore all broken hearts,
Slay grief, and let sweet consolation in,-
Turn thou thyself.
If thou would'st cure the world
Of its long sickness, end its grief and pain;
Bring in all-healing joy,
And give to the afflicted rest again,-
Then cure thyself.
If thou would'st wake the world
Out of its dream of death and dark'ning strife,
Bring it to Love and Peace,
And Light and brightness of immortal Life,-
Wake thou thyself.

3. THE WAY OUT OF UNDESIRABLE CONDITIONS

Having seen and realized that evil is but a passing shadow thrown, by the intercepting self, across the transcendent Form of the Eternal Good, and that the world is a mirror in which each sees a reflection of himself, we now ascend, by firm and easy steps, to that plane of perception whereon is seen and realized the Vision of the Law.

With this realization comes the knowledge that everything is included in a ceaseless interaction of cause and effect, and that nothing can possibly be divorced from law.

From the most trivial thought, word, or act of man, up to the groupings of the celestial bodies, law reigns supreme. No arbitrary condition can, even for one moment, exist, for such a condition would be a denial and an annihilation of law.

Every condition of life is, therefore, bound up in an orderly and harmonious sequence, and the secret and cause of every condition is contained within itself, The law, "Whatsoever a man sows that shall he also reap," is inscribed in flaming letters upon the portal of Eternity, and none can deny it, none can cheat it, none can escape it.

He who puts his hand in the fire must suffer the burning until such time as it has worked itself out, and neither curses nor prayers can avail to alter it.

And precisely the same law governs the realm of mind. Hatred, anger, jealousy, envy, lust, covetousness, all these are fires which bum, and whoever even so much as touches them must suffer the torments of burning.

All these conditions of mind are rightly called "evil," for they are the efforts of the soul to subvert, in its ignorance, the law, an they, therefore, lead to chaos and confusion within, and are sooner or later actualized in the outward circumstances as disease, failure, and misfortune, coupled with grief, pain, and despair.

Whereas love, gentleness, good-will, purity, are cooling airs which breathe peace upon the soul that woes them, and, being in harmony with the Eternal Law, they become actualized in the form of health, peaceful surroundings, and undeviating success and good fortune.

A thorough understanding of this Great Law which permeates the universe leads to the acquirement of that state of mind known as obedience.

To know that justice, harmony, and love are supreme in the universe is likewise to know that all adverse and painful conditions are the result of our own disobedience to that Law.

Such knowledge leads to strength and power, and it is upon such knowledge alone that a true life and an enduring success and happiness can be built.

To be patient under all circumstances, and to accept all conditions as necessary factors in your training, is to rise superior to all painful conditions, and to overcome them with an overcoming which is sure, and which leaves no fear of their return, for by the power of obedience to law they are utterly slain.

Such an obedient one is working in harmony with the law, has in fact, identified himself with the law, and whatsoever he conquers he conquers for ever, whatsoever he builds can never be destroyed.

The cause of all power, as of all weakness, is within; the secret of all happiness as of all misery is likewise within.

There is no progress apart from unfoldment within, and no sure foothold of prosperity or peace except by orderly advancement in knowledge.

You say you are chained by circumstances; you cry out for better opportunities, for a wider scope, for improved physical conditions, and perhaps you inwardly curse the fate that binds you hand and foot.

It is for you that I write; it is to you that I speak. Listen, and let my words burn themselves into your heart, for that which I say to you is truth:

You may bring about that improved condition in your outward life which you desire, if you will unswervingly resolve to improve your inner life.

I know this pathway looks barren at its commencement (truth always does, it is only error and delusion which are at first inviting and fascinating,) but if you undertake to walk it; if you perseveringly discipline your mind, eradicating your weaknesses, and allowing your soul-forces and spiritual powers to unfold themselves, you will be astonished at the magical changes which will be brought about in your outward life.

As you proceed, golden opportunities will be strewn across your path, and the power and judgment to properly utilize them will spring up within you. Genial friends will come unbidden to you; sympathetic souls will be drawn to you as the needle is to the magnet; and books and all outward aids that you require will come to you unsought.

Perhaps the chains of poverty hang heavily upon you, and you are friendless and alone, and you long with an intense longing that your load may be lightened; but the load continues, and you seem to be enveloped in an ever-increasing darkness.

Perhaps you complain, you bewail your lot; you blame your birth, your parents, your employer, or the unjust Powers who have bestowed upon you so undeservedly poverty and hardship, and upon another affluence and ease.

Cease your complaining and fretting; none of these things which you blame are the cause of your poverty; the cause is within yourself, and where the cause is, there is the remedy.

The very fact that you are a complainer, shows that you deserve your lot; shows that you lack that faith which is the ground of all effort and progress.

There is no room for a complainer in a universe of law, and worry is soul-suicide. By your very attitude of mind you are strengthening the chains which bind you, and are drawing about you the darkness by which you are enveloped, Alter your outlook upon life, and your outward life will alter.

Build yourself up in the faith and knowledge, and make yourself worthy of better surroundings and wider opportunities. Be sure, first of all, that you are making the best of what you have.

Do not delude yourself into supposing that you can step into greater advantages whilst overlooking smaller ones, for if you could, the advantage would be impermanent and you would quickly fall back again in order to learn the lesson which you had neglected.

As the child at school must master one standard before passing onto the next, so, before you can have that greater good which you so desire, must you faithfully employ that which you already possess.

The parable of the talents is a beautiful story illustrative of this truth, for does it not plainly show that if we misuse, neglect, or degrade that which we possess, be it ever so mean and insignificant, even that little will be taken from us, for, by our conduct we show that we are unworthy of it.

Perhaps you are living in a small cottage, and are surrounded by unhealthy and vicious influences.

You desire a larger and more sanitary residence. Then you must fit yourself for such a residence by first of all making your cottage as far as possible a little paradise. Keep it spotlessly clean. Make it look as pretty and sweet as your limited means will allow. Cook your plain food with all care, and arrange your humble table as tastefully as you possibly can.

If you cannot afford a carpet, let your rooms be carpeted with smiles and welcomes, fastened down with the nails of kind words driven in with the hammer of
patience. Such a carpet will not fade in the sun, and constant use will never wear it away.

By so ennobling your present surroundings you will rise above them, and above the need of them, and at the right time you will pass on into the better house and surroundings which have all along been waiting for you, and which you have fitted yourself to occupy.

Perhaps you desire more time for thought and effort, and feel that your hours of labor are too hard and long. Then see to it that you are utilizing to the fullest possible extent what little spare time you have.

It is useless to desire more time, if you are already wasting what little you have; for you would only grow more indolent and indifferent.

Even poverty and lack of time and leisure are not the evils that you imagine they are, and if they hinder you in your progress, it is because you have clothed them in your own weaknesses, and the evil that you see in them is really in yourself. Endeavor to fully and completely realize that in so far as you shape and mould your mind, you are the maker of your destiny, and as, by the transmuting power of self-discipline you realize this more and more, you will come to see that these so-called evils may be converted into blessings.

You will then utilize your poverty for the cultivation of patience, hope and courage; and your lack of time in the gaining of promptness of action and decision of mind, by seizing the precious moments as they present themselves for your acceptance.

As in the rankest soil the most beautiful flowers are grown, so in the dark soil of poverty the choicest flowers of humanity have developed and bloomed.

Where there are difficulties to cope with, and unsatisfactory conditions to overcome, there virtue most flourishes and manifests its glory.

It may be that you are in the employ of a tyrannous master or mistress, and you feel that you are harshly treated. Look upon this also as necessary to your training. Return your employer's unkindness with gentleness and forgiveness.

Practice unceasingly patience and self-control. Turn the disadvantage to account by utilizing it for the gaining of mental and spiritual strength, and by your silent example and influence you will thus be teaching your employer, will be helping him to grow ashamed of his conduct, and will, at the same time, be lifting yourself up to that height of spiritual attainment by which you will be enabled to step into new and more congenial surroundings at the time when they are presented to you.

Do not complain that you are a slave, but lift yourself up, by noble conduct, above the plane of slavery. Before complaining that you are a slave to another, be sure that you are not a slave to self.

Look within; look searchingly, and have no mercy upon yourself. You will find there, perchance, slavish thoughts, slavish desires, and in your daily life and conduct slavish habits.

Conquer these; cease to be a slave to self, and no man will have the power to enslave you. As you overcome self, you will overcome all adverse conditions, and every difficulty will fall before you.

Do not complain that you are oppressed by the rich. Are you sure that if you gained riches you would not be an oppressor yourself?

Remember that there is the Eternal Law which is absolutely just, and that he who oppresses today must himself be oppressed tomorrow; and from this there is no way of escape.

And perhaps you, yesterday (in some former existence) were rich and an oppressor, and that you are now merely paying off the debt which you owe to the Great Law. Practice, therefore, fortitude and faith.

Dwell constantly in mind upon the Eternal justice, the Eternal Good. Endeavor to lift yourself above the personal and the transitory into the impersonal and permanent.

Shake off the delusion that you are being injured or oppressed by another, and try to realize, by a profounder comprehension of your inner life, and the laws which govern that life, that you are only really injured by what is within you. There is no practice more degrading, debasing, and soul-destroying than that of self-pity.

Cast it out from you. While such a canker is feeding upon your heart you can never expect to grow into a fuller life.

Cease from the condemnation of others, and begin to condemn yourself. Condone none of your acts, desires or thoughts that will not bear comparison with spotless purity, or endure the light of sinless good.

By so doing you will be building your house upon the rock of the Eternal, and all that is required for your happiness and well-being will come to you in its own time.

There is positively no way of permanently rising above poverty, or any undesirable condition, except by eradicating those selfish and negative conditions within, of which these are the reflection, and by virtue of which they continue.

The way to true riches is to enrich the soul by the acquisition of virtue. Outside of real heart-virtue there is neither prosperity nor power, but only the appearances of these. I am aware that men make money who have acquired no measure of virtue, and have little desire to do so; but such money does not constitute true riches, and its possession is transitory and feverish.

Here is David's testimony:- For I was envious at the foolish when I saw the prosperity of the wicked...... Their eyes stand out with fatness; they have more than heart could wish. -Verily I have cleansed my heart in vain, and washed my hands in innocence... When I thought to know this it was too painful for me; until I went into the sanctuary of God, then understood I their end."

The prosperity of the wicked was a great trial to David until he went into the sanctuary of God, and then he knew their end.

You likewise may go into that sanctuary. It is within you. It is that state of consciousness which remains when all that is sordid, and personal, and impermanent is risen above, and universal and eternal principles are realized.

That is the God state of consciousness; it is the sanctuary of the Most High. When by long strife and self-discipline, you have succeeded in entering the door of that holy Temple, you will perceive, with unobstructed vision, the end and fruit of all human thought and endeavor, both good and evil.

You will then no longer relax your faith when you see the immoral man accumulating outward riches, for you will know, that he must come again to poverty and degradation.

The rich man who is barren of virtue is, in reality, poor, and as surely, as the waters of the river are drifting to the ocean, so surely is he, in the midst of all his riches, drifting towards poverty and misfortune; and though he die rich, yet must he return to reap the bitter fruit of all of his immorality.

And though he become rich many times, yet as many times must he be thrown back into poverty, until, by long experience and suffering he conquers the poverty within.

But the man who is outwardly poor, yet rich in virtue, is truly rich, and, in the midst of all his poverty he is surely traveling towards prosperity; and abounding joy and bliss await his coming. If you would become truly and permanently prosperous, you must first become virtuous.

It is therefore unwise to aim directly at prosperity, to make it the one object of life, to reach out greedily for it, To do this is to ultimately defeat yourself.

But rather aim at self-perfection, make useful and unselfish service the object of your life, and ever reach out hands of faith towards the supreme and unalterable Good.

You say you desire wealth, not for your own sake, but in order to do good with it, and to bless others. If this is your real motive in desiring wealth, then wealth will come to you; for you are strong and unselfish indeed if, in the midst of riches, you are willing to look upon yourself as steward and not as owner.

But examine well your motive, for in the majority of instances where money is desired for the admitted object of blessing others, the real underlying motive is a love of popularity, and a desire to pose as a philanthropist or reformer.

If you are not doing good with what little you have, depend upon it the more money you got the more selfish you would become, and all the good you appeared to do with your money, if you attempted to do any, would be so much insinuating self-laudation.

If your real desire is to do good, there is no need to wait for money before you do it; you can do it now, this very moment, and just where you are. If you are really so unselfish as you believe yourself to be, you will show it by sacrificing yourself for others now.

No matter how poor you are, there is room for self-sacrifice, for did not the widow put her all into the treasury?

The heart that truly desires to do good does not wait for money before doing it, but comes to the altar of sacrifice and, leaving there the unworthy elements of self, goes out and breathes upon neighbor and stranger, friend and enemy alike the breath of blessedness.

As the effect is related to the cause, so is prosperity and power related to the inward good and poverty and weakness to the inward evil.

Money does not constitute true wealth, nor position, nor power, and to rely upon it alone is to stand upon a slippery place.

20

Your true wealth is your stock of virtue, and your true power the uses to which you put it. Rectify your heart, and you will rectify your life. Lust, hatred, anger, vanity, pride, covetousness, self-indulgence, self-seeking, obstinacy,- all these are poverty and weakness; whereas love, purity, gentleness, meekness, compassion, generosity, self-forgetfulness, and self-renunciation,- all these are wealth and power.

As the elements of poverty and weakness are overcome, an irresistible and allconquering power is evolved from within, and he who succeeds in establishing himself in the highest virtue, brings the whole world to his feet.

But the rich, as well as the poor, have their undesirable conditions, and are frequently farther removed from happiness than the poor. And here we see how happiness depends, not upon outward aids or possessions, but upon the inward life.

Perhaps you are an employer, and you have endless trouble with those whom you employ, and when you do get good and faithful servants they quickly leave you. As a result you are beginning to lose, or have completely lost, your faith in human nature.

You try to remedy matters by giving better wages, and by allowing certain liberties, yet matters remain unaltered. Let me advise you.

The secret of all your trouble is not in your servants, it is in yourself; and if you look within, with a humble and sincere desire to discover and eradicate your error, you will, sooner or later, find the origin of all your unhappiness.

It may be some selfish desire, or lurking suspicion, or unkind attitude of mind which sends out its poison upon those about you, and reacts upon yourself, even though you may not show it in your manner or speech.

Think of your servants with kindness, consider of them that extremity of service which you yourself would not care to perform were you in their place.

Rare and beautiful is that humility of soul by which a servant entirely forgets himself in his master's good; but far rarer, and beautiful with a divine beauty, is that nobility of soul by which a man, forgetting his own happiness, seeks the happiness of those who are under his authority, and who depend upon him for their bodily sustenance.

And such a man's happiness is increased tenfold, nor does he need to complain of those whom he employs. Said a well known and extensive employer of labor, who never needs to dismiss an employee: "I have always had the happiest relations with my workpeople.

If you ask me how it is to be accounted for, I can only say that it has been my aim from the first to do to them as I would wish to be done by." Herein lies the secret by which all desirable conditions are secured, and all that are undesirable are overcome.

Do you say that you are lonely and unloved, and have "not a friend in the world"? Then, I pray you, for the sake of your own happiness, blame nobody but yourself.

Be friendly towards others, and friends will soon flock round you. Make yourself pure and lovable, and you will be loved by all.

Whatever conditions are rendering your life burdensome, you may pass out of and beyond them by developing and utilizing within you the transforming power of self-purification and self-conquest.

Be it the poverty which galls (and remember that the poverty upon which I have been dilating is that poverty which is a source of misery, and not that voluntary poverty which is the glory of emancipated souls), or the riches which burden, or the many misfortunes, griefs, and annoyances which form the dark background in the web of life, you may overcome them by overcoming the selfish elements within which give them life.

It matters not that by the unfailing Law, there are past thoughts and acts to work out and to atone for, as, by the same law, we are setting in motion, during every moment of our life, fresh thoughts and acts, and we have the power to make them good or ill.

Nor does it follow that if a man (reaping what he has sown) must lose money or forfeit position, that he must also lose his fortitude or forfeit his uprightness, and it is in these that his wealth and power and happiness are to be found. He who clings to self is his own enemy and is surrounded by enemies.

He who relinquishes self is his own savior, and is surrounded by friends like a protecting belt. Before the divine radiance of a pure heart all darkness vanishes and all clouds melt away, and he who has conquered self has conquered the universe.

Come, then, out of your poverty; come out of your pain; come out of your troubles, and sighings, and complainings, and heartaches, and loneliness by coming out of yourself.

Let the old tattered garment of your petty selfishness fall from you, and put on the new garment of universal Love. You will then realize the inward heaven, and it will be reflected in all your outward life.

He who sets his foot firmly upon the path of self-conquest, who walks, aided by the staff of Faith, the highway of self-sacrifice, will assuredly achieve the highest prosperity, and will reap abounding and enduring joy and bliss.

> To them that seek the highest good
> All things subserve the wisest ends;
> Nought comes as ill, and wisdom lends
> Wings to all shapes of evil brood.
> The dark'ning sorrow veils a Star
> That waits to shine with gladsome light;
> Hell waits on heaven; and after night
> Comes golden glory from afar.

Defeats are steps by which we climb
With purer aim to nobler ends;
Loss leads to gain, and joy attends
True footsteps up the hills of time.
Pain leads to paths of holy bliss,
To thoughts and words and deeds divine-,
And clouds that gloom and rays that shine,
Along life's upward highway kiss.
Misfortune does but cloud the way
Whose end and summit in the sky
Of bright success, sunkiss'd and high,
Awaits our seeking and our stay.
The heavy pall of doubts and fears
That clouds the Valley of our hopes,
The shades with which the spirit copes,
The bitter harvesting of tears,
The heartaches, miseries, and griefs,
The bruisings born of broken ties,
All these are steps by which we rise
To living ways of sound beliefs.
Love, pitying, watchful, runs to meet
The Pilgrim from the Land of Fate;
All glory and all good await
The coming of obedient feet.

4. THE SILENT POWER OF THOUGHT: CONTROLLING AND DIRECTING ONE'S FORCES

The most powerful forces in the universe are the silent forces; and in accordance with the intensity of its power does a force become beneficent when rightly directed, and destructive when wrongly employed.

This is a common knowledge in regard to the mechanical forces, such as steam, electricity, etc., but few have yet learned to apply this knowledge to the realm of mind, where the thought-forces (most powerful of all) are continually being generated and sent forth as currents of salvation or destruction.

At this stage of his evolution, man has entered into the possession of these forces, and the whole trend of his present advancement is their complete subjugation. All the wisdom possible to man on this material earth is to be found only in complete self-mastery, and the command, "Love your enemies," resolves itself into an exhortation to enter here and now, into the possession of that sublime wisdom by taking hold of, mastering and transmuting, those mind forces to which man is now slavishly subject, and by which he is helplessly borne, like a straw on the stream, upon the currents of selfishness.

The Hebrew prophets, with their perfect knowledge of the Supreme Law, always related outward events to inward thought, and associated national disaster or success with the thoughts and desires that dominated the nation at the time.

The knowledge of the causal power of thought is the basis of all their prophecies, as it is the basis of all real wisdom and power. National events are simply the working out of the psychic forces of the nation.

Wars, plagues, and famines are the meeting and clashing of wrongly-directed thought-forces, the culminating points at which destruction steps in as the agent of the Law.

It is foolish to ascribe war to the influence of one man, or to one body of men. It is the crowning horror of national selfishness. It is the silent and conquering thought-forces which bring all things into manifestation.

The universe grew out of thought. Matter in its last analysis is found to be merely objectivized thought. All men's accomplishments were first wrought out in thought, and then objectivized.

The author, the inventor, the architect, first builds up his work in thought, and having perfected it in all its parts as a complete and harmonious whole upon the thought-plane. he then commences to materialize it, to bring it down to the material or sense-plane.

When the thought-forces are directed in harmony with the over-ruling Law, they are up-building and preservative, but when subverted they become disintegrating and self-destructive.

To adjust all your thoughts to a perfect and unswerving faith in the omnipotence and supremacy of Good, is to co-operate with that Good, and to realize within yourself the solution and destruction of all evil. Believe and ye shall live.

And here we have the true meaning of salvation; salvation from the darkness and negation of evil, by entering into, and realizing the living light of the Eternal Good.

Where there is fear, worry, anxiety, doubt, trouble, chagrin, or disappointment, there is ignorance and lack of faith.

All these conditions of mind are the direct outcome of selfishness, and are based upon an inherent belief in the power and supremacy of evil; they therefore constitute practical atheism; and to live in, and become subject to, these negative and soul-destroying conditions of mind is the only real atheism.

It is salvation from such conditions that the race needs, and let no man boast of salvation whilst he is their helpless and obedient slave.

To fear or to worry is as sinful as to curse, for how can one fear or worry if he intrinsically believes in the Eternal justice, the Omnipotent Good, the Boundless Love? To fear, to worry, to doubt, is to deny, to dis-believe.

It is from such states of mind that all weakness and failure proceed, for they represent the annulling and disintegrating of the positive thought-forces which would otherwise speed to their object with power, and bring about their own beneficent results.

To overcome these negative conditions is to enter into a life of power, is to cease to be a slave, and to become a master, and there is only one way by which they can be overcome, and that is by steady and persistent growth in inward knowledge.

To mentally deny evil is not sufficient; it must, by daily practice, be risen above and understood. To mentally affirm the good is inadequate; it must, by unswerving endeavor, be entered into and comprehended.

The intelligent practice of self-control, quickly leads to a knowledge of one's interior thought-forces, and, later on, to the acquisition of that power by which they are rightly employed and directed.

In the measure that you master self, that you control your mental forces instead of being controlled by them, in just such measure will you master affairs and outward circumstances.

Show me a man under whose touch everything crumbles away, and who cannot retain success even when it is placed in his hands, and I will show you a man who dwells continually in those conditions of mind which are the very negation of power.

To be for ever wallowing in the bogs of doubt, to be drawn continually into the quicksands of fear, or blown ceaselessly about by the winds of anxiety, is to be a slave, and to live the life of a slave, even though success and influence be for ever knocking at your door seeking for admittance.

Such a man, being without faith and without self-government, is incapable of the right government of his affairs, and is a slave to circumstances; in reality a slave to himself. Such are taught by affliction, and ultimately pass from weakness to strength by the stress of bitter experience. Faith and purpose constitute the motive- power of life.

There is nothing that a strong faith and an unflinching purpose may not accomplish. By the daily exercise of silent faith, the thought-forces are gathered together, and by the daily strengthening of silent purpose, those forces are directed toward the object of accomplishment.

Whatever your position in life may be, before you can hope to enter into any measure of success, usefulness, and power, you must learn how to focus your thought-forces by cultivating calmness and repose. It may be that you are a business man, and you are suddenly confronted with some overwhelming difficulty or probable disaster. You grow fearful and anxious, and are at your wit's end.

To persist in such a state of mind would be fatal, for when anxiety steps in, correct judgment passes out. Now if you will take advantage of a quiet hour or two in the early morning or at night, and go away to some solitary spot, or to some room in your house where you know you will be absolutely free from intrusion, and, having seated yourself in an easy attitude, you forcibly direct your mind right away from the object of anxiety by dwelling upon something in your life that is pleasing and blissgiving, a calm, reposeful strength will gradually steal into your mind, and your anxiety will pass away.

Upon the instant that you find your mind reverting to the lower plane of worry bring it back again, and re-establish it on the plane of peace and strength.

When this is fully accomplished, you may then concentrate your whole mind upon the solution of your difficulty, and what was intricate and insurmountable to you in your hour of anxiety will be made plain and easy, and you will see, with that clear vision and perfect judgment which belong only to a calm and untroubled mind, the right course to pursue and the proper end to be brought about.

It may be that you will have to try day after day before you will be able to perfectly calm your mind, but if you persevere you will certainly accomplish it. And the course which is presented to you in that hour of calmness must be carried out.

Doubtless when you are again involved in the business of the day, and worries again creep in and begin to dominate you, you will begin to think that the course is a wrong or foolish one, but do not heed such suggestions.

Be guided absolutely and entirely by the vision of calmness, and not by the shadows of anxiety. The hour of calmness is the hour of illumination and correct judgment.

By such a course of mental discipline the scattered thought-forces are re-united, and directed, like the rays of the search-light, upon the problem at issue, with the result that it gives way before them.

There is no difficulty, however great, but will yield before a calm and powerful concentration of thought, and no legitimate object but may be speedily actualized by the intelligent use and direction of one's soul-forces.

Not until you have gone deeply and searchingly into your inner nature, and have overcome many enemies that lurk there, can you have any approximate conception of the subtle power of thought, of its inseparable relation to outward and material things, or of its magical potency, when rightly poised and directed, in readjusting and transforming the life-conditions.

Every thought you think is a force sent out, and in accordance with its nature and intensity will it go out to seek a lodgment in minds receptive to it, and will react upon yourself for good or evil. There is ceaseless reciprocity between mind and mind, and a continual interchange of thought-forces.

Selfish and disturbing thoughts are so many malignant and destructive forces, messengers of evil, sent out to stimulate and augment the evil in other minds, which in turn send them back upon you with added power.

While thoughts that are calm, pure, and unselfish are so many angelic messengers sent out into the world with health, healing, and blessedness upon their wings, counteracting the evil forces; pouring the oil of joy upon the troubled waters of anxiety and sorrow, and restoring to broken hearts their heritage of immortality.

Think good thoughts, and they will quickly become actualized in your outward life in the form of good conditions. Control your soul-forces, and you will be able to shape your outward life as you will.

The difference between a savior and a sinner is this, that the one has a perfect control of all the forces within him; the other is dominated and controlled by them.

There is absolutely no other way to true power and abiding peace, but by self-control, self-government, self-purification. To be at the mercy of your disposition is to be impotent, unhappy, and of little real use in the world.

The conquest of your petty likes and dislikes, your capricious loves and hates, your fits of anger, suspicion, jealousy, and all the changing moods to which you are more or less helplessly subject, this is the task you have before you if you would weave into the web of life the golden threads of happiness and prosperity.

In so far as you are enslaved by the changing moods within you, will you need to depend upon others and upon outward aids as you walk through life.

If you would walk firmly and securely, and would accomplish any achievement, you must learn to rise above and control all such disturbing and retarding vibrations.

You must daily practice the habit of putting your mind at rest, "going into the silence," as it is commonly called. This is a method of replacing a troubled thought with one of peace, a thought of weakness with one of strength.

Until you succeed in doing this you cannot hope to direct your mental forces upon the problems and pursuits of life with any appreciable measure of success. It is a process of diverting one's scattered forces into one powerful channel.

Just as a useless marsh may be converted into a field of golden corn or a fruitful garden by draining and directing the scattered and harmful streams into one wellcut channel, so, he who acquires calmness, and subdues and directs the thoughtcurrents within himself, saves his soul, and fructifies his heart and life.

As you succeed in gaining mastery over your impulses and thoughts you will begin to feel, growing up within you, a new and silent power, and a settled feeling of composure and strength will remain with you.

Your latent powers will begin to unfold themselves, and whereas formerly your efforts were weak and ineffectual, you will now be able to work with that calm confidence which commands success.

And along with this new power and strength, there will be awakened within you that interior Illumination known as "intuition," and you will walk no longer in darkness and speculation, but in light and certainty.

With the development of this soul-vision, judgment and mental penetration will be incalculably increased, and there will evolve within you that prophetic vision by the aid of which you will be able to sense coming events, and to forecast, with remarkable accuracy, the result of your efforts.

And in just the measure that you alter from within will your outlook upon life alter; and as you alter your mental attitude towards others they will alter in their attitude and conduct toward you.

As you rise above the lower, debilitating, and destructive thought-forces, you will come in contact with the positive, strengthening, and up-building currents generated by strong, pure, and noble minds, your happiness will be immeasurably intensified, and you will begin to realize the joy, strength, and power, which are born only of self-mastery.

And this joy, strength, and power will be continually radiating from you, and without any effort on your part, nay, though you are utterly unconscious of it, strong people will be drawn toward you, influence will be put into your hands, and in accordance with your altered thought-world will outward events shape themselves.

"A man's foes are they of his own household," and he who would be useful, strong, and happy, must cease to be a passive receptacle for the negative, beggardly, and impure streams of thought; and as a wise householder commands his servants and invites his guests, so must he learn to command his desires, and to say, with authority, what thoughts he shall admit into the mansion of his soul.

Even a very partial success in self-mastery adds greatly to one's power, and he who succeeds in perfecting this divine accomplishment, enters into possession of undreamed-of wisdom and inward strength and peace, and realizes that all the forces of the universe aid and protect his footsteps who is master of his soul.

Would you scale the highest heaven,
Would you pierce the lowest hell,
Live in dreams of constant beauty,
Or in basest thinkings dwell.
For your thoughts are heaven above you,
And your thoughts are hell below,
Bliss is not, except in thinking,
Torment nought but thought can know.
Worlds would vanish but for thinking;
Glory is not but in dreams;
And the Drama of the ages
From the Thought Eternal streams.
Dignity and shame and sorrow,
Pain and anguish, love and hate
Are but maskings of the mighty
Pulsing Thought that governs Fate.
As the colors of the rainbow
Makes the one uncolored beam,
So the universal changes
Make the One Eternal Dream.
And the Dream is all within you,
And the Dreamer waiteth long
For the Morning to awake him
To the living thought and strong.
That shall make the ideal real,
Make to vanish dreams of hell
In the highest, holiest heaven
Where the pure and perfect dwell.
Evil is the thought that thinks it;
Good, the thought that makes it so

Light and darkness, sin and pureness
Likewise out of thinking grow.
Dwell in thought upon the Grandest,
And the Grandest you shall see ;
Fix your mind upon the Highest,
And the Highest you shall be.

5. THE SECRET OF HEALTH, SUCCESS AND POWER

We all remember with what intense delight, as children, we listened to the nevertiring fairy-tale. How eagerly we followed the fluctuating fortunes of the good boy or girl, ever protected, in the hour of crisis, from the evil machinations of the scheming witch, the cruel giant, or the wicked king.

And our little hearts never faltered for the fate of the hero or heroine, nor did we doubt their ultimate triumph over all their enemies, for we knew that the fairies were infallible, and that they would never desert those who had consecrated themselves to the good and the true.

And what unspeakable joy pulsated within us when the Fairy-Queen, bringing all her magic to bear at the critical moment, scattered all the darkness and trouble, and granted them the complete satisfaction of all their hopes, and they were "happy ever after."

With the accumulating years, and an ever-increasing intimacy with the so-called "realities" of life, our beautiful fairy-world became obliterated, and its wonderful inhabitants were relegated, in the archives of memory, to the shadowy and unreal.

And we thought we were wise and strong in thus leaving for ever the land of childish dreams, but as we re-become little children in the wondrous world of wisdom, we shall return again to the inspiring dreams of childhood and find that they are, after all, realities.

The fairy-folk, so small and nearly always invisible, yet possessed of an all-conquering and magical power, who bestow upon the good, health, wealth, and happiness, along with all the gifts of nature in lavish profusion, start again into reality and become immortalized in the soul-realm of him who, by growth in wisdom, has entered into a knowledge of the power of thought, and the laws which govern the inner world of being.

To him the fairies live again as thought-people, thought-messengers, thoughtpowers working in harmony with the over-ruling Good. And they who, day by day, endeavor to harmonize their hearts with the heart of the Supreme Good, do in reality acquire true health, wealth, and happiness.

There is no protection to compare with goodness, and by "goodness" I do not mean a mere outward conformity to the rules of morality; I mean pure thought, noble aspiration, unselfish love, and freedom from vainglory.

To dwell continually in good thoughts, is to throw around oneself a psychic atmosphere of sweetness and power which leaves its impress upon all who come in contact with it.

As the rising sun puts to rout the helpless shadows, so are all the impotent forces of evil put to flight by the searching rays of positive thought which shine forth from a heart made strong in purity and faith.

Where there is sterling faith and uncompromising purity there is health, there is success, there is power. In such a one, disease, failure, and disaster can find no lodgment, for there is nothing on which they can feed.

Even physical conditions are largely determined by mental states, and to this truth the scientific world is rapidly being drawn.

The old, materialistic belief that a man is what his body makes him, is rapidly passing away, and is being replaced by the inspiring belief that man is superior to his body, and that his body is what he makes it by the power of thought.

Men everywhere are ceasing to believe that a man is despairing because he is dyspeptic, and are coming to understand that he is dyspeptic because he is despairing, and in the near future, the fact that all disease has its origin in the mind will become common knowledge.

There is no evil in the universe but has its root and origin in the mind, and sin, sickness, sorrow, and affliction do not, in reality, belong to the universal order, are not inherent in the nature of things, but are the direct outcome of our ignorance of the right relations of things.

According to tradition, there once lived, in India, a school of philosophers who led a life of such absolute purity and simplicity that they commonly reached the age of one hundred and fifty years, and to fall sick was looked upon by them as an unpardonable disgrace, for it was considered to indicate a violation of law.

The sooner we realize and acknowledge that sickness, far from being the arbitrary visitation of an offended God, or the test of an unwise Providence, is the result of our own error or sin, the sooner shall we enter upon the highway of health.

Disease comes to those who attract it, to those whose minds and bodies are receptive to it, and flees from those whose strong, pure, and positive thought-sphere generates healing and life-giving currents.

If you are given to anger, worry, jealousy, greed, or any other inharmonious state of mind, and expect perfect physical health, you are expecting the impossible, for you are continually sowing the seeds of disease in your mind.

Such conditions of mind are carefully shunned by the wise man, for he knows them to be far more dangerous than a bad drain or an infected house.

If you would be free from all physical aches and pains, and would enjoy perfect physical harmony, then put your mind in order, and harmonize your thoughts. Think joyful thoughts; think loving thoughts; let the elixir of goodwill course through your veins, and you will need no other medicine. Put away your jealousies, your suspicions, your worries, your hatreds, your selfish indulgences, and you will put away your dyspepsia, your biliousness, your nervousness and aching joints.

If you will persist in clinging to these debilitating and demoralizing habits of mind, then do not complain when your body is laid low with sickness. The following story illustrates the close relation that exists between habits of mind and bodily conditions.

A certain man was afflicted with a painful disease, and he tried one physician after another, but all to no purpose. He then visited towns which were famous for their curative waters, and after having bathed in them all, his disease was more painful than ever.

One night he dreamed that a Presence came to him and said, "Brother, hast thou tried all the means of cure?" and he replied, "I have tried all." "Nay," said the Presence, "Come with me, and I will show thee a healing bath which has escaped thy notice."

The afflicted man followed, and the Presence led him to a clear pool of water, and said, "Plunge thyself in this water and thou shalt surely recover," and thereupon vanished.

The man plunged into the water, and on coming out, lo! his disease had left him, and at the same moment he saw written above the pool the word "Renounce." Upon waking, the full meaning of his dream flashed across his mind, and looking within he discovered that he had, all along, been a victim to a sinful indulgence, and he vowed that he would renounce it for ever.

He carried out his vow, and from that day his affliction began to leave him, and in a short time he was completely restored to health. Many people complain that they have broken down through over-work. In the majority of such cases the breakdown is more frequently the result of foolishly wasted energy.

If you would secure health you must learn to work without friction. To become anxious or excited, or to worry over needless details is to invite a breakdown.

Work, whether of brain or body, is beneficial and health-giving, and the man who can work with a steady and calm persistency, freed from all anxiety and worry, and with his mind utterly oblivious to all but the work he has in hand, will not only accomplish far more than the man who is always hurried and anxious, but he will retain his health, a boon which the other quickly forfeits.

True health and true success go together, for they are inseparably intertwined in the thought-realm. As mental harmony produces bodily health, so it also leads to a harmonious sequence in the actual working out of one's plans.

Order your thoughts and you will order your life. Pour the oil of tranquility upon the turbulent waters of the passions and prejudices, and the tempests of misfortune, howsoever they may threaten, will be powerless to wreck the barque of your soul, as it threads its way across the ocean of life.

And if that barque be piloted by a cheerful and never-failing faith its course will be doubly sure, and many perils will pass it by which would otherwise attack it.

By the power of faith every enduring work is accomplished. Faith in the Supreme; faith in the over-ruling Law; faith in your work, and in your power to accomplish that work, -here is the rock upon which you must build if you would achieve, if you would stand and not fall.

To follow, under all circumstances, the highest promptings within you; to be always true to the divine self; to rely upon the inward Light, the inward Voice, and to pursue your purpose with a fearless and restful heart, believing that the future will yield unto you the meed of every thought and effort; knowing that the laws of the universe can never fail, and that your own will come back to you with mathematical exactitude, this is faith and the living of faith.

By the power of such a faith the dark waters of uncertainty are divided, every mountain of difficulty crumbles away, and the believing soul passes on unharmed.

Strive, O reader! to acquire, above everything, the priceless possession of this dauntless faith, for it is the talisman of happiness, of success, of peace, of power, of all that makes life great and superior to suffering.

Build upon such a faith, and you build upon the Rock of the Eternal, and with the materials of the Eternal, and the structure that you erect will never be dissolved, for it will transcend all the accumulations of material luxuries and riches, the end of which is dust.

Whether you are hurled into the depths of sorrow or lifted upon the heights of joy, ever retain your hold upon this faith, ever return to it as your rock of refuge, and keep your feet firmly planted upon its immortal and immovable base.

Centered in such a faith, you will become possessed of such a spiritual strength as will shatter, like so many toys of glass, all the forces of evil that are hurled against you, and you will achieve a success such as the mere striver after worldly gain can never know or even dream of. "If ye have faith, and doubt not, ye shall not only do this, ... but if ye shall say unto this mountain, be thou removed and be thou cast into the sea, it shall be done."

There are those today, men and women tabernacled in flesh and blood, who have realized this faith, who live in it and by it day by day, and who, having put it to the uttermost test, have entered into the possession of its glory and peace.

Such have sent out the word of command, and the mountains of sorrow and disappointment, of mental weariness and physical pain have passed from them, and have been cast into the sea of oblivion.

If you will become possessed of this faith you will not need to trouble about your success or failure, and success will come.

You will not need to become anxious about results, but will work joyfully and peacefully, knowing that right thoughts and right efforts will inevitably bring about right results.

I know a lady who has entered into many blissful satisfactions, and recently a friend remarked to her, "Oh, how fortunate you are! You only have to wish for a thing, and it comes to you."

And it did, indeed, appear so on the surface; but in reality all the blessedness that has entered into this woman's life is the direct outcome of the inward state of blessedness which she has, throughout life, been cultivating and training toward perfection.

Mere wishing brings nothing but disappointment; it is living that tells.

The foolish wish and grumble; the wise, work and wait. And this woman had worked; worked without and within, but especially within upon heart and soul; and with the invisible hands of the spirit she had built up, with the precious stones of faith, hope, joy, devotion, and love, a fair temple of light, whose glorifying radiance was ever round about her.

It beamed in her eye; it shone through her countenance; it vibrated in her voice; and all who came into her presence felt its captivating spell.

And as with her, so with you. Your success, your failure, your influence, your whole life you carry about with you, for your dominant trends of thought are the determining factors in your destiny.

Send forth loving, stainless, and happy thoughts, and blessings will fall into your hands, and your table will be spread with the cloth of peace.

Send forth hateful, impure, and unhappy thoughts, and curses will rain down upon you, and fear and unrest will wait upon your pillow. You are the unconditional maker of your fate, be that fate what it may. Every moment you are sending forth from you the influences which will make or mar your life.

Let your heart grow large and loving and unselfish, and great and lasting will be your influence and success, even though you make little money.

Confine it within the narrow limits of self-interest, and even though you become a millionaire your influence and success, at the final reckoning will be found to be utterly insignificant. Cultivate, then, this pure and unselfish spirit, and combine with purity and faith, singleness of purpose, and you are evolving from within the elements, not only of abounding health and enduring success, but of greatness and power.

If your present position is distasteful to you, and your heart is not in your work, nevertheless perform your duties with scrupulous diligence, and whilst resting your mind in the idea that the better position and greater opportunities are waiting for you, ever keep an active mental outlook for budding possibilities, so that when the critical moment arrives, and the new channel presents itself, you will step into it with your mind fully prepared for the undertaking, and with that intelligence and foresight which is born of mental discipline.

Whatever your task may be, concentrate your whole mind upon it, throw into it all the energy of which you are capable. The faultless completion of small tasks leads inevitably to larger tasks. See to it that you rise by steady climbing, and you will never fall. And herein lies the secret of true power.

Learn, by constant practice, how to husband your resources, and to concentrate them, at any moment, upon a given point. The foolish waste all their mental and spiritual energy in frivolity, foolish chatter, or selfish argument, not to mention wasteful physical excesses.

If you would acquire overcoming power you must cultivate poise and passivity. You must be able to stand alone. All power is associated with immovability. The mountain, the massive rock, the storm-tried oak, all speak to us of power, because of their combined solitary grandeur and defiant fixity; while the shifting sand, the yielding twig, and the waving reed speak to us of weakness, because they are movable and non-resistant, and are utterly useless when detached from their fellows.

He is the man of power who, when all his fellows are swayed by some emotion or passion, remains calm and unmoved. He only is fitted to command and control who has succeeded in commanding and controlling himself.

The hysterical, the fearful, the thoughtless and frivolous, let such seek company, or they will fall for lack of support; but the calm, the fearless, the thoughtful, and let such seek the solitude of the forest, the desert, and the mountain-top, and to their power more power will be added, and they will more and more successfully stem the psychic currents and whirlpools which engulf mankind.

Passion is not power; it is the abuse of power, the dispersion of power. Passion is like a furious storm which beats fiercely and wildly upon the embattled rock whilst power is like the rock itself, which remains silent and unmoved through it all.

That was a manifestation of true power when Martin Luther, wearied with the persuasions of his fearful friends, who were doubtful as to his safety should he go to Worms, replied, "If there were as many devils in Worms as there are tiles on the housetops I would go."

And when Benjamin Disraeli broke down in his first Parliamentary speech, and brought upon himself the derision of the House, that was an exhibition of germinal power when he exclaimed, "The day will come when you will consider it an honor to listen to me."

When that young man, whom I knew, passing through continual reverses and misfortunes, was mocked by his friends and told to desist from further effort, and he replied, "The time is not far distant when you will marvel at my good fortune and success," he showed that he was possessed of that silent and irresistible power which has taken him over innumerable difficulties, and crowned his life with success.

If you have not this power, you may acquire it by practice, and the beginning of power is likewise the beginning of wisdom. You must commence by overcoming those purposeless trivialities to which you have hitherto been a willing victim.

Boisterous and uncontrolled laughter, slander and idle talk, and joking merely to raise a laugh, all these things must be put on one side as so much waste of valuable energy.

St. Paul never showed his wonderful insight into the hidden laws of human progress to greater advantage than when he warned the Ephesians against "Foolish talking and jesting which is not convenient," for to dwell habitually in such practices is to destroy all spiritual power and life.

As you succeed in rendering yourself impervious to such mental dissipations you will begin to understand what true power is, and you will then commence to grapple with the more powerful desires and appetites which hold your soul in bondage, and bar the way to power, and your further progress will then be made clear.

Above all be of single aim; have a legitimate and useful purpose, and devote yourself unreservedly to it. Let nothing draw you aside ; remember that the doubleminded man is unstable in all his ways.

Be eager to learn, but slow to beg. Have a thorough understanding of your work, and let it be your own; and as you proceed, ever following the inward Guide, the infallible Voice, you will pass on from victory to victory, and will rise step by step to higher resting-places, and your ever-broadening outlook will gradually reveal to you the essential beauty and purpose of life.

Self-purified, health will be yours; faith-protected, success will be yours; self-governed, power will be yours, and all that you do will prosper, for, ceasing to be a disjointed unit, self-enslaved, you will be in harmony with the Great Law, working no longer against, but with, the Universal Life, the Eternal Good.

And what health you gain it will remain with you; what success you achieve will be beyond all human computation, and will never pass away; and what influence and power you wield will continue to increase throughout the ages, for it will be a part of that unchangeable Principle which supports the universe.

This, then, is the secret of health, -a pure heart and a well-ordered mind ; this is the secret of success, -an unfaltering faith, and a wisely-directed purpose; and to rein in, with unfaltering will, the dark steed of desire, this is the secret of power.

All ways are waiting for my feet to tread,
The light and dark, the living and the dead,
The broad and narrow way, the high and low,
The good and bad, and with quick step or slow,
I now may enter any way I will,
And find, by walking, which is good, which ill.
And all good things my wandering feet await,
If I but come, with vow inviolate,
Unto the narrow, high and holy way
Of heart-born purity, and therein stay;
Walking, secure from him who taunts and scorns,
To flowery meads, across the path of thorns.
And I may stand where health, success, and power
Await my coming, if, each fleeting hour,
I cling to love and patience; and abide
With stainlessness; and never step aside
From high integrity ; so shall I see
At last the land of immortality.
And I may seek and find; I may achieve,
I may not claim, but, losing, may retrieve.
The law bends not for me, but I must bend
Unto the law, if I would reach the end
Of my afflictions, if I would restore
My soul to Light and Life, and weep no more.
Not mine the arrogant and selfish claim
To all good things; be mine the lowly aim
To seek and find, to know and comprehend,
And wisdom-ward all holy footsteps wend,
Nothing is mine to claim or to command,
But all is mine to know and understand.

6. THE SECRET OF ABOUNDING HAPPINESS

Great is the thirst for happiness, and equally great is the lack of happiness. The majority of the poor long for riches, believing that their possession would bring them supreme and lasting happiness.

Many who are rich, having gratified every desire and whim, suffer from ennui and repletion, and are farther from the possession of happiness even than the very poor.

If we reflect upon this state of things it will ultimately lead us to a knowledge of the all important truth that happiness is not derived from mere outward possessions, nor misery from the lack of them; for if this were so, we should find the poor always miserable, and the rich always happy, whereas the reverse is frequently the case.

Some of the most wretched people whom I have known were those who were surrounded with riches and luxury, whilst some of the brightest and happiest people I have met were possessed of only the barest necessities of life.

Many men who have accumulated riches have confessed that the selfish gratification which followed the acquisition of riches has robbed life of its sweetness, and that they were never so happy as when they were poor.

What, then, is happiness, and how is it to be secured? Is it a figment, a delusion, and is suffering alone perennial? We shall find, after earnest observation and reflection, that all, except those who have entered the way of wisdom, believe that happiness is only to be obtained by the gratification of desire.

It is this belief, rooted in the soil of ignorance, and continually watered by selfish cravings, that is the cause of all the misery in the world.

And I do not limit the word desire to the grosser animal cravings; it extends to the higher psychic realm, where far more powerful, subtle, and insidious cravings hold in bondage the intellectual and refined, depriving them of all that beauty, harmony, and purity of soul whose expression is happiness.

Most people will admit that selfishness is the cause of all the unhappiness in the world, but they fall under the soul-destroying delusion that it is somebody else's selfishness, and not their own.

When you are willing to admit that all your unhappiness is the result of your own selfishness you will not be far from the gates of Paradise; but so long as you are convinced that it is the selfishness of others that is robbing you of joy, so long will you remain a prisoner in your self-created purgatory.

Happiness is that inward state of perfect satisfaction which is joy and peace, and from which all desire is eliminated. The satisfaction which results from gratified desire is brief and illusionary, and is always followed by an increased demand for gratification.

Desire is as insatiable as the ocean, and clamors louder and louder as its demands are attended to.

It claims ever-increasing service from its deluded devotees, until at last they are struck down with physical or mental anguish, and are hurled into the purifying fires of suffering. Desire is the region of hell, and all torments are centered there.

The giving up of desire is the realization of heaven, and all delights await the pilgrim there,

I sent my soul through the invisible,
Some letter of that after life to spell,
And by-and-by my soul returned to me,
And whispered, I myself am heaven and hell,"

Heaven and hell are inward states. Sink into self and all its gratifications, and you sink into hell; rise above self into that state of consciousness which is the utter denial and forgetfulness of self, and you enter heaven.

Self is blind, without judgment, not possessed of true knowledge, and always leads to suffering. Correct perception, unbiased judgment, and true knowledge belong only to the divine state, and only in so far as you realize this divine consciousness can you know what real happiness is.

So long as you persist in selfishly seeking for your own personal happiness, so long will happiness elude you, and you will be sowing the seeds of wretchedness.

In so far as you succeed in losing yourself in the service of others, in that measure will happiness come to you, and you will reap a harvest of bliss.

It is in loving, not in being loved,
The heart is blessed;
It is in giving, not in seeking gifts,
We find our quest.
Whatever be thy longing or thy need,
That do thou give;
So shall thy soul be fed, and thou indeed
Shalt truly live.

Cling to self, and you cling to sorrow, relinquish self, and you enter into peace. To seek selfishly is not only to lose happiness, but even that which we believe to be the source of happiness.

See how the glutton is continually looking about for a new delicacy wherewith to stimulate his deadened appetite; and how, bloated, burdened, and diseased, scarcely any food at last is eaten with pleasure.

Whereas, he who has mastered his appetite, and not only does not seek, but never thinks of gustatory pleasure, finds delight in the most frugal meal. The angel-form of happiness, which men, looking through the eyes of self, imagine they see in gratified desire, when clasped is always found to be the skeleton of misery. Truly, "He that seeketh his life shall lose it, and he that loseth his life shall find it."

Abiding happiness will come to you when, ceasing to selfishly cling, you are willing to give up. When you are willing to lose, unreservedly, that impermanent thing which is so dear to you, and which, whether you cling to it or not, will one day be snatched from you, then you will find that that which seemed to you like a painful loss, turns out to be a supreme gain.

To give up in order to gain, than this there is no greater delusion, nor no more prolific source of misery; but to be willing to yield up and to suffer loss, this is indeed the Way of Life.

How is it possible to find real happiness by centering ourselves in those things which, by their very nature, must pass away? Abiding and real happiness can only be found by centering ourselves in that which is permanent.

Rise, therefore, above the clinging to and the craving for impermanent things, and you will then enter into a consciousness of the Eternal, and as, rising above self, and by growing more and more into the spirit of purity, self-sacrifice and universal Love, you become centered in that consciousness, you will realize that happiness which has no reaction, and which can never be taken from you.

The heart that has reached utter self-forgetfulness in its love for others has not only become possessed of the highest happiness but has entered into immortality, for it has realized the Divine.

Look back upon your life, and you will find that the moments of supremest happiness were those in which you uttered some word, or performed some act, of compassion or self-denying love. Spiritually, happiness and harmony are, synonymous.

Harmony is one phase of the Great Law whose spiritual expression is love. All selfishness is discord, and to be selfish is to be out of harmony with the Divine order.

As we realize that all-embracing love which is the negation of self, we put ourselves in harmony with the divine music, the universal song, and that ineffable melody which is true happiness becomes our own.

Men and women are rushing hither and thither in the blind search for happiness, and cannot find it; nor ever will until they recognize that happiness is already within them and round about them, filling the universe, and that they, in their selfish searching are shutting themselves out from it.

I followed happiness to make her mine,
Past towering oak and swinging ivy vine.
She fled, I chased, o'er slanting hill and dale,
O'er fields and meadows, in the purpling vale;
Pursuing rapidly o'er dashing stream.
I scaled the dizzy cliffs where eagles scream;
I traversed swiftly every land and M.
But always happiness eluded me.
Exhausted, fainting, I pursued no more,
But sank to rest upon a barren shore.
One came and asked for food, and one for alms
I placed the bread and gold in bony palms.
One came for sympathy, and one for rest;
I shared with every needy one my best;
When, Io! sweet Happiness, with form divine,
Stood by me, whispering softly, 'I am thine'.

These beautiful lines of Burleigh's express the secret of all abounding happiness. Sacrifice the personal and transient, and you rise at once into the impersonal and permanent.

Give up that narrow cramped self that seeks to render all things subservient to its own petty interests, and you will enter into the company of the angels, into the very heart and essence of universal Love.

Forget yourself entirely in the sorrows of others and in ministering to others, and divine happiness will emancipate you from all sorrow and suffering.

"Taking the first step with a good thought, the second with a good word, and the third with a good deed, I entered Paradise." And you also may enter into Paradise by pursuing the same course. It is not beyond, it is here. It is realized only by the unselfish.

It is known in its fullness only to the pure in heart. If you have not realized this unbounded happiness you may begin to actualize it by ever holding before you the lofty ideal of unselfish love, and aspiring towards it.

Aspiration or prayer is desire turned upward. It is the soul turning toward its Divine source, where alone permanent satisfaction can be found. By aspiration the destructive forces of desire are transmuted into divine and all-preserving energy.

To aspire is to make an effort to shake off the trammels of desire; it is the prodigal made wise by loneliness and suffering, returning to his Father's Mansion.

As you rise above the sordid self; as you break, one after another, the chains that bind you, will you realize the joy of giving, as distinguished from the misery of grasping - giving of your substance; giving of your intellect; giving of the love and light that is growing within you.

You will then understand that it is indeed "more blessed to give than to receive." But the giving must be of the heart without any taint of self, without desire for reward. The gift of pure love is always attended with bliss. If, after you have given, you are wounded because you are not thanked or flattered, or your name put in the paper, know then that your gift was prompted by vanity and not by love, and you were merely giving in order to get; were not really giving, but grasping.

Lose yourself in the welfare of others; forget yourself in all that you do; this is the secret of abounding happiness.

Ever be on the watch to guard against selfishness, and learn faithfully the divine lessons of inward sacrifice; so shall you climb the highest heights of happiness, and shall remain in the neverclouded sunshine of universal joy, clothed in the shining garment of immortality.

Are you searching for the happiness that does not fade away?
Are you looking for the joy that lives, and leaves no grievous day?
Are you panting for the waterbrooks of Love, and Life, and Peace?
Then let all dark desires depart, and selfish seeking cease.
Are you ling'ring in the paths of pain, grief-haunted, stricken sore?
Are you wand'ring in the ways that wound your weary feet the more?
Are you sighing for the Resting-Place where tears and sorrows cease?
Then sacrifice your selfish heart and find the Heart of Peace.

7. THE REALIZATION OF PROSPERITY

It is granted only to the heart that abounds with integrity, trust, generosity and love to realize true prosperity. The heart that is not possessed of these qualities cannot know prosperity, for prosperity, like happiness, is not an outward possession, but an inward realization.

The greedy man may become a millionaire, but he will always be wretched, and mean, and poor, and will even consider himself outwardly poor so long as there is a man in the world who is richer than himself, whilst the upright, the open-handed and loving will realize a full and rich prosperity, even though their outward possessions may be small.

He is poor who is dissatisfied; he is rich who is contented with what he has, and he is richer who is generous with what he has.

When we contemplate the fact that the universe is abounding in all good things, material as well as spiritual, and compare it with man's blind eagerness to secure a few gold coins, or a few acres of dirt, it is then that we realize how dark and ignorant selfishness is; it is then that we know that self-seeking is self-destruction.

Nature gives all, without reservation, and loses nothing; man, grasping all, loses everything.

If you would realize true prosperity do not settle down, as many have done, into the belief that if you do right everything will go wrong. Do not allow the word "competition" to shake your faith in the supremacy of righteousness.

I care not what men may say about the "laws of competition," for do I not know the unchangeable Law, which shall one day put them all to rout, and which puts them to rout even now in the heart and life of the righteous man?

And knowing this Law I can contemplate all dishonesty with undisturbed repose, for I know where certain destruction awaits it. Under all circumstances do that which you believe to be right, and trust the Law; trust the Divine Power that is imminent in the universe, and it will never desert you, and you will always be protected.

By such a trust all your losses will be converted into gains, and all curses which threaten will be transmuted into blessings. Never let go of integrity, generosity, and love, for these, coupled with energy, will lift you into the truly prosperous state.

Do not believe the world when it tells you that you must always attend to "number one" first, and to others afterwards. To do this is not to think of others at all, but only of one's own comforts.

To those who practice this the day will come when they will be deserted by all, and when they cry out in their loneliness and anguish there will be no one to hear and help them. To consider one's self before all others is to cramp and warp and hinder every noble and divine impulse.

Let your soul expand, let your heart reach out to others in loving and generous warmth, and great and lasting will be your joy, and all prosperity will come to you. Those who have wandered from the highway of righteousness guard themselves against competition; those who always pursue the right need not to trouble about such defense.

This is no empty statement, There are men today who, by the power of integrity and faith, have defied all competition, and who, without swerving in the least from their methods, when competed with, have risen steadily into prosperity, whilst those who tried to undermine them have fallen back defeated.

To possess those inward qualities which constitute goodness is to be armored against all the powers of evil, and to be doubly protected in every time of trial; and to build' oneself up in those qualities is to build up a success which cannot be shaken, and to enter into a prosperity which will endure forever.

> The White Robe of the Heart Invisible
> Is stained with sin and sorrow, grief and pain,
> And all repentant pools and springs of prayer
> Shall not avail to wash it white again.
> While in the path of ignorance I walk,
> The stains of error will not cease to cling
> Defilements mark the crooked path of self,
> Where anguish lurks and disappointments sting.
> Knowledge and wisdom only can avail
> To purify and make my garment clean,
> For therein lie love's waters ; therein rests
> Peace undisturbed, eternal, and serene.
> Sin and repentance is the path of pain,
> Knowledge and wisdom is the path of Peace
> By the near way of practice I will find
> Where bliss begins, how pains and sorrows cease.
> Self shall depart, and Truth shall take its place
> The Changeless One, the Indivisible
> Shall take up His abode in me, and cleanse
> The White Robe of the Heart Invisible.

Made in the USA
Columbia, SC
15 February 2019